HUMAN RIGHTS AT RISK

MODERN SLAVERY AND HUMAN TRAFFICKING

by Gail Radley

BrightPoint Press

San Diego, CA

© 2025 BrightPoint Press
an imprint of ReferencePoint Press, Inc.
Printed in the United States

For more information, contact:
BrightPoint Press
PO Box 27779
San Diego, CA 92198
www.BrightPointPress.com

ALL RIGHTS RESERVED.

No part of this work covered by the copyright hereon may be reproduced or used in any form or by any means—graphic, electronic, or mechanical, including photocopying, recording, taping, web distribution, or information storage retrieval systems—without the written permission of the publisher.

LIBRARY OF CONGRESS CATALOGING-IN-PUBLICATION DATA

Names: Radley, Gail, author.
Title: Modern slavery and human trafficking / by Gail Radley.
Description: San Diego, CA: BrightPoint Press, [2025] | Series: Human rights at risk | Includes bibliographical references and index. | Audience: Grades 7-9
Identifiers: LCCN 2024004135 (print) | LCCN 2024004136 (eBook) | ISBN 9781678209285 (hardcover) | ISBN 9781678209292 (eBook)
Subjects: LCSH: Slavery--History--21st century. | Human trafficking.
Classification: LCC HT867.R34 2025 (print) | LCC HT867 (eBook) | DDC 306.3/62--dc23/eng/20240314
LC record available at https://lccn.loc.gov/2024004135
LC eBook record available at https://lccn.loc.gov/2024004136

CONTENTS

AT A GLANCE	4
INTRODUCTION ADRIANA'S STORY	6
CHAPTER ONE SEX TRAFFICKING	12
CHAPTER TWO FORCED LABOR	22
CHAPTER THREE DEBT AND DESCENT SLAVERY	34
CHAPTER FOUR ENDING SLAVERY	44
Glossary	58
Source Notes	59
For Further Research	60
Index	62
Image Credits	63
About the Author	64

AT A GLANCE

- Modern enslaved people are people who are robbed of their freedom and forced to work with little to no pay. They are also called victims of human trafficking.

- Slavery exists around the world, including in the United States. The United Nations (UN) believes that about 50 million people were enslaved in 2021.

- Two main types of modern slavery are sex slavery and forced labor.

- Some traffickers groom victims to gain their trust. They encourage victims to become dependent on them in order to abuse them.

- Common targets for traffickers include young people, migrants, people of color, and people who are experiencing poverty and other hardships.

- Millions of people are kept in slavery by debt. They are paid little to nothing for their work, making it nearly impossible to earn their freedom. Their children may inherit their debt.

- Traffickers look for potential victims on social media and gaming sites. They scan these sites to gather information about those they target.

- Ending slavery requires the cooperation of all countries. Businesses and individuals also have important roles to play.

INTRODUCTION

ADRIANA'S STORY

Adriana dreamed of beautiful clothes, flashy cars, and a fancy lifestyle. She was a 13-year-old runaway and needed money. A smooth-talking man promised it all. Soon, the man's name was tattooed across her chest. It made Adriana feel like she belonged. But it meant he owned her. She couldn't make her own choices anymore.

Young girls who leave home in search of a better life are especially vulnerable to human trafficking.

Adriana had been trafficked. A trafficked person is someone who is forced to work or sell sex. They are no longer free. They no longer have control over their lives. This is a form of modern slavery.

At first, victims may think they are bettering their lives. But their trafficker gets their pay. Adriana's new life meant selling sex to strangers all night. It meant beatings if she didn't earn enough. It sometimes meant breaking other laws for her trafficker, too. Victims might be told to steal or hide drugs. They have little choice but to do it.

There is no easy way out of this life. "You have no idea how I am breaking inside," Adriana told a reporter years later.[1] Some victims mask their pain with drugs. Others die by suicide or are killed.

Young people who have been trafficked or enslaved may cope with their situation by using drugs.

WHAT ARE TRAFFICKING AND MODERN SLAVERY?

When people think of slavery, they may think of US history. Slavery existed in some colonies since the country was founded. In the South, it lasted through the mid-1800s. The American Civil War (1861–1865) ended that type of slavery in the United States. But slavery actually

Through the centuries, slavery has been practiced in nearly all parts of the world.

began before written history. It has been robbing people of their freedom for thousands of years.

In the 2020s slavery is still found in nearly every country, including the United States. The true number of **enslaved** people isn't known. They often live and work beside free people. Fearing their traffickers, they keep quiet. The United Nations (UN) believes that about 50 million people were enslaved in 2021. That was more than the number of students in US public schools that year.

CHAPTER ONE

SEX TRAFFICKING

Most human trafficking is for sex. Some victims are trafficked close to home. Others are sent far away. The United States is among the countries with the most victims. Victims live in both cities and rural areas.

One way to understand the size of this problem is to count calls made to hotlines. These are phone numbers people can call to get help. In the United States,

Many human trafficking victims are forced to have sex for money. In 2022, this number was 6 million people.

anyone with information about trafficking can call the National Human Trafficking Hotline. The hotline got tips on nearly 10,360 suspected cases in 2021. One case can have many victims. The International Labour Organization (ILO) published a report, *Global Estimates of Modern Slavery*, in 2022. It estimated that some 6 million people worldwide were enslaved for sex.

    Many, like Adriana, have run away from home. Traffickers target them. They know most runaways need money for food and shelter. When basic needs aren't met, it's easy to believe traffickers' lies. People lacking power and privilege often become targets. Young people in foster care and people who aren't citizens are also likely targets.

Traffickers are able to win over teens who may be living on the streets with promises of food, clothing, and a warm place to sleep.

Most sex trafficking victims are adults. Many were first trafficked as minors. Most victims are females, but males are sex trafficked as well.

HOW IT HAPPENS

Victims are often tricked into trusting someone they shouldn't. This process is called **grooming**. A girl might meet a man at a party or the mall. Soon, she thinks he is a friend or boyfriend. He promises to take care of her. He draws her away from friends and family. She learns to rely on him. When he's happy with her, she feels safe and loved.

The more she relies on him, the more control he has. He makes rules. If she

Young girls may be willing to trust men who buy them things and make them feel loved.

doesn't obey, he becomes angry and violent. He might torture her, threaten her family, and withhold food. If she becomes addicted to drugs, she is easy to control. To get drugs, she must do what he says. In time, she will do anything to keep him calm.

Most sex traffickers are male. But women take part, too. They could be the traffickers' girlfriends or family. Women may find victims for male traffickers. They might manage the business. Sometimes the women begin as enslaved sex workers and then create their own sex slave business. This is more common outside the United States. The women succeed because some people trust women more than men. Women are also less likely to be arrested.

Some victims are forced to sell sex to strangers on the street. Others work out of bars or hotels. Spas and massage parlors can be **fronts** for selling sex. Victims might also be forced to pose for photos or act in adult movies. These may be posted on the internet.

Ghislaine Maxwell

Ghislaine Maxwell was 58 when she was charged with bringing teens as young as 14 to her friend, Jeffrey Epstein, for sexual assault. Sometimes, Maxwell joined in. A victim called her "cruel and merciless."[3] In 2022, she was sentenced to 20 years in prison.

Source: Lauren Del Valle, Mark Morales, Sonia Moghe, and Eric Levenson. "Ghislaine Maxwell Sentenced to 20 Years in Prison for Sex Trafficking Minor Girls for Jeffrey Epstein," CNN, *June 28, 2022. www.cnn.com.*

FORCED MARRIAGE

Many women and girls become enslaved through forced marriage. This is not the same as an arranged marriage. In arranged marriages, people agree to let their parents or someone else choose their partner.

But sometimes arranged marriages are actually forced. Families may insist on marriage. Or parents may promise to give their child in marriage later. Even a child may be married. Parents may threaten to disown children who won't obey. They may beat them.

In some countries, women have little control over their lives. Forced marriage is more common in such places. If a woman runs away from her husband, she often has

Women's organizations around the world protest child marriages.

nowhere to turn for help. Even the law may work against her.

Forced marriages are also common where people are very poor. A family may think marriage will give their child a better life. They may even sell one of their children and use the money to buy food for the other children. "I was 12 years old when I got married to a 35-year-old man," said Gloria, age 17.[2] She thought he would help her family once they married. He did not.

Someone who forces a partner into marriage isn't likely to agree to a divorce. Some countries restrict or don't allow divorce. A 2022 report by the ILO suggests that some 22 million women and girls live in forced marriages worldwide.

When marriage is forced, victims' partners become their enslavers. The victim must obey the partner. Many of these victims are enslaved for sex. They may also be forced to work. So, there isn't always a clear line between sex slavery and the other major type of modern slavery, forced labor.

CHAPTER TWO

FORCED LABOR

One day, a 14-year-old South African girl learned that her family was making her marry a stranger. No one asked what she wanted. The 28-year-old man had seen her on the street. He liked her looks. He paid her family for her. Her schooling ended. He enslaved her. When she ran away, men in her family returned her. The girl and her enslaver lived with his brother and sister-in-law. The girl had to do all the

Modern slavery can be hard to spot. It's difficult to know if someone who cooks and cleans in a private home is hired to do so or if they are enslaved.

cooking and cleaning. She was kept locked inside. In the end, this girl was lucky. Her enslaver was finally sentenced to prison.

Customs and even laws can work against girls in some countries. But in other countries, people may be shocked to learn that slavery is nearby. Angela Me studies crime and drugs for the UN. She notes that people may think modern slavery happens only in faraway countries. They may know that traffickers prey on people whose lives are uprooted for some reason, such as a war. But, she says, "It can also happen next door."[3]

Some families in wealthy countries hire domestic workers to work inside the home. They may be hired to clean, cook, and care for children. Sometimes they live at work.

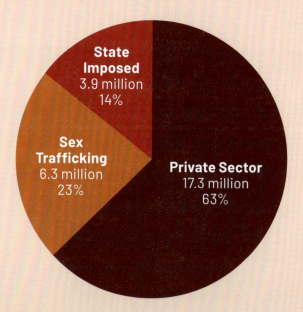

Source: *"Global Estimates of Modern Slavery: Forced Labour and Forced Marriage,"* International Labour Organization, September 2022. www.ilo.org.

In 2021 the total number of people in forced labor worldwide was 27.5 million. Most worked in the private sector, including people's homes.

From the outside, it can be hard to know if a domestic worker is enslaved. It may look like the person is simply an employee. Sometimes what began as a lawful job may turn into slavery. This is particularly true with a live-in job. Some domestic workers are on call 24 hours a day. They are unable to leave and are always expected to be working. They can't go anywhere without asking. They lose track of family and friends. Their whole world becomes the family they work for.

Some are locked in as the South African teenager was. Some are beaten. They may be paid little or nothing. The family may say the worker is paid with free room and board. The worker can't move to another job. Slavery robs these workers of choices.

MIGRANT WORKERS AND FORCED LABOR

Migrant workers move from place to place, working short-term jobs. They may work in factories, farms, or mines. Some are construction workers or fishermen.

In some parts of the world, young boys and girls are forced into working long days in construction without proper gear.

Most migrants lack skills for stable jobs. Some work in their own countries. Others travel to different countries for work. Leaving their homelands makes them immigrants as well as migrants.

Both migrants and immigrants are likely targets for traffickers. The problem

27

is worldwide. In the United States, 55 percent of the victims reported to the National Human Trafficking Hotline in 2021 were immigrants. Thousands of Mexicans and Central Americans are caught in forced labor in the United States each year. Usually, they are smuggled into the country. Some trafficked workers enter legally. But traffickers take away their legal papers. They abuse them and threaten their families.

The workers don't know whom to trust. Kara Napolitano is a manager at Laboratory to Combat Human Trafficking (LCHT). "Labor trafficking survivors don't often report because they are afraid, don't understand what's happened to them is trafficking, and don't know to whom or how to report," she explains.[4]

Migrant workers from Mexico and other Latin American countries are sometimes victims of trafficking. They may be brought into the United States to work without payment.

COVID-19 PANDEMIC

The COVID-19 pandemic was a worldwide health crisis. It created new problems and made old ones worse. Millions became sick, and millions died. Those who could work from home did so. Businesses lost customers. Some shut down for good. People lost their jobs. Others were forced to keep working. These included medical, drugstore, and grocery workers. Companies that made face masks, gloves, and other medical supplies suddenly had more orders than they could fill. They needed more workers fast.

Migrants and other poor people faced great hardships. With workers scarce, some companies drifted into forced labor. These companies demanded longer work hours. Others made their workers stay on-site. With more people homebound, violence against live-in workers also rose. Other domestic workers lost their jobs and became homeless.

Slowly, things seemed to return to normal. But the poverty rate stayed high. In 2022, some 75 to 95 million more people in the world lived in deep poverty than before the pandemic. This left millions more as possible targets for traffickers.

In 2021, the ILO reported that over 27 million people were likely doing forced labor. At that time, the world was still gripped by the pandemic. About 6 million women were forced laborers.

Child Soldiers

Younis was about 12 years old when rebels forced him to fight in Yemen's civil war. He was badly wounded. Finally, he escaped and returned to his family. United Nations International Children's Emergency Fund (UNICEF) reports that over 105,000 children were made to fight, act as spies or cooks, or do other work during the wars that lasted from 2005 to 2022. Some were only 8 or 9 years old.

Almost twice as many men, 11.3 million, were in forced labor jobs. Children made up about 1.3 million. That number is slightly less than the total population of Philadelphia, Pennsylvania, in 2023.

Some forced laborers fall into yet another category. They appear to have paying jobs. But they are working to pay off huge debts. The little they receive is not enough to support them and pay the debts. As a result, they are caught in debt or descent slavery.

The pandemic pushed many into poverty around the world. In the United States, the number of people who could no longer afford rent meant an increase in urban encampments.

CHAPTER THREE

DEBT AND DESCENT SLAVERY

Puspal couldn't stay home a day while ill. She knew her debt would grow. Puspal worked at a brick kiln in India. This is a big oven where workers fire bricks. The work is hot and dangerous. Workers breathe in black smoke all day. Two workers ran away. They were caught, locked up, and beaten. The boss wouldn't let them leave until their debt was paid. The debt was 60,000 rupees, about $724.

Young women and men work long hours in the brick kilns of India. They fire bricks and then carry and stack them by hand.

In nearby Pakistan, Yasmin was caught in the same trap. "It wasn't by choice," she said. It was a hard time. Her husband fell ill. They couldn't buy medicine. Other family members died. "[H]ousehold expenses and other problems forced me to take this route," she added.[5] Yasmin made about six dollars daily. If she didn't make 1,000 bricks each day, she lost pay. Borrowing three dollars meant paying back six dollars. She had been making bricks for 10 years. This debt is a form of slavery. Millions of people are caught up in this cycle. They make up one-fifth of forced labor victims. The debt-enslaved often live where they work. They must pay for food, water, and housing.

Most victims live in South Asia. Many make bricks. Others work on farms or in mills, mines, or factories. Others are construction workers. As with other forms of modern slavery, most victims were poor and powerless before being enslaved. They lived at the edge of crisis. They had no savings to see them through. Banks would

Forced labor is common in clothing factories in Southeast Asia. People work long hours for little pay.

not help. Their own labor was all they had to offer.

SLAVERY PAST AND PRESENT

The term *modern slavery* suggests it is different from past slavery. It is true that there are differences. In the 2020s, slavery is illegal. Most people oppose slavery. But today's slavery is similar to historical slavery in some important ways.

Starting in the early 1500s, settlers from Europe enslaved Africans and brought them to North America. They also enslaved native people. These days traffickers prey on people of color and migrants. These groups have higher rates of poverty than others. Debt slavery relies on the poverty of its victims.

The enslaved, past or present, are constantly shown that they don't matter. Profits grow when they are pushed beyond their limits. Enslavers spend as little as possible on their workers. Food is limited and cheap. Medical care is rare. Housing is often crowded shacks with few comforts. Insects and rats may share their space. Safety is ignored. Workers seldom have protective gear for dangerous jobs.

Slavery in Georgia

One of the biggest human trafficking cases in the United States involved dozens of traffickers in 2023. They had **lured** more than 200 Mexicans and Central Americans to Georgia. The workers were promised good farming jobs. But they were enslaved to pick blueberries. They were given dirty, unsafe housing and little food.

The very poor in India are often victims of descent slavery. Deep debt may force them to live wherever they can find shelter.

In US slavery before the Civil War, an enslaved woman's children were enslaved as well. They might be given jobs by age 3. Most modern enslaved people aren't born into slavery. But when a debt worker falls behind, family pitches in. Eleven-year-old Qaiser of Pakistan loved school. He wanted to become a doctor. When his father fell ill, Qaiser had to quit school. He worked from sunrise to 8:00 p.m. Debt may be passed on endlessly from parent to child.

DESCENT SLAVERY

Some people are born into slavery, not through debt but through tradition. This is descent slavery. Descent slavery is deeply woven into north-central Africa's culture. It looks much like early US slavery.

The last country to outlaw slavery was Mauritania in 1981. But slavery continued there. About 20 percent of the population is enslaved. Hundreds of years ago, lighter-skinned Moors raided villages in Mauritania. The darker-skinned Africans were defeated. They became enslaved. Slave status passed from mother to child. The enslaved are taught that their slavery is natural. Accepting slavery may even be built into religion. Over time, people begin to believe what they're told.

Learning that they deserve better lives can take time. What can be even harder is finding a way toward that better life. Creating those opportunities is part of the answer. So is putting an end to slavery in all its forms.

In Mauritania, darker-skinned people are discriminated against, as they are formerly enslaved people. Some work dangerous jobs in gold mines to make ends meet.

CHAPTER FOUR

ENDING SLAVERY

In 2015 the UN set seventeen goals to improve life throughout the world. One goal is to end all forms of child slavery by 2025. All countries in the UN agreed to it. Walk Free is an anti-slavery organization. It reports that the United States works harder to find and help victims of modern slavery than any other country. The United Kingdom, Australia, the Netherlands, and

Activists around the world are doing their part to draw attention to the need to end modern slavery.

Portugal are among the other nations working to end modern slavery.

Progress has been made. But the ILO argues that changes haven't gone far enough to meet the goals. By 2018, advances slowed. Wars, climate change, and other problems stood in the way. The COVID-19 pandemic slowed progress even more. And the demand for enslaved people has increased.

NATIONS RESPOND

The UN can set goals to end slavery, but nations must take action. In the United States, for example, victims get physical and mental health care. They are given legal help. Job training and housing help guide them to build new lives. Individual nations

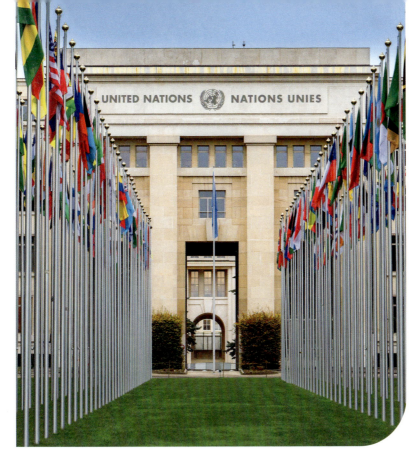

The UN has established conventions to end modern slavery, but individual nations must end slavery within their own borders as well.

must also educate the public. Once victims are free, some countries help create the programs. A task force helps US programs work together. The country's wealth makes funding the efforts possible.

Yet slavery continues in the United States and elsewhere. Countries with the lowest numbers of enslaved people still have thousands of forced marriages and laborers. Gaps in the laws and lack of enforcement get some of the blame. Sometimes minors are arrested for selling sex, but their traffickers escape punishment. Traffickers are good at finding loopholes in laws and weak points in processes. Some countries allow forced marriage. There are even US states that allow it. A few states allow marriage at any age. And even in the United States, laws meant to protect migrant workers don't stop trafficking.

ECONOMIC ACTION

Even as they fight slavery, many countries take actions that keep it alive. Wealthy countries like the United States **import** goods from poor countries. Forced labor may be used to grow raw materials, make the goods, and ship the finished products. This is often the case with electronics, cloth products, palm oil, and solar panels. These are at-risk goods, meaning they are made with forced labor.

China **exports** more goods than any other country. China's Xinjiang area is well known for forced labor. In 2022 the

Victim Turned Hero

A trafficker groomed 13-year-old Alicia Kozakiewicz online. After gaining her trust, the person she thought was a boy talked her into meeting him near her Pittsburgh home. He was 38, and he abducted her. With therapy, Kozakiewicz recovered. As an adult, she fights slavery by teaching others to spot its signs.

United States passed a law that stopped shipments from Xinjiang from entering the country. US agents stopped thousands of shipments in the first year. And yet some still get through. At the same time, Europe is importing more goods from Xinjiang. The United States also imports some at-risk goods. In 2022 it imported nearly $170 billion worth of at-risk goods.

No nation has succeeded in buying only goods made by free workers. As the biggest importer of goods, the United States can do a lot to fight forced labor. But nations need to work together.

Businesses can fight slavery by not buying goods made with forced labor. For example, certain divisions of Lindt, Hershey's, and Mars make sure that workers at their suppliers are free and treated fairly. The words *fair trade* are noted on such products. Customers can push other companies to do the right thing. Forced labor will end if people stop buying

Factories in the Xinjiang province of China routinely use forced labor to produce goods that are shipped to consumers around the world.

goods made by enslaved people. Some antislavery groups offer lists of fair trade, or freely made, products. End Slavery Now is among them.

RECOGNIZING SLAVERY

Modern enslaved people are often afraid to report what's happened to them. But others can learn the signs of an enslaved person. Then they can report it.

A person being sent somewhere against their will may look afraid. Someone may watch them closely in public. They may be afraid to talk to other people. This includes the police or others who might help. The person might be traveling with few belongings and no identification. They may appear not to know where they are or

People who are being trafficked may be wearing clothes that are out of season. They may appear to be lost and have few belongings.

where they're going. Children may seem drunk or drugged. They may also have scars, bruises, and burns.

Enslaved people may be taken to jobs and picked up at odd times. They may wear the same clothing daily. Their clothes may seem wrong for the place or activity. They may be dressed in poorly fitting clothing. Or they may be wearing clothes that don't fit the season.

It is best not to question someone who may be enslaved. Instead, the police or someone in charge should be told. Calling the National Trafficking Hotline at 888-373-7888 can help. As CNN writer Francesca Street puts it, "Seeing something and reporting it could . . . keep someone from becoming a victim of modern slavery."[6]

ONLINE TRAFFICKING

Many young people use social media and gaming sites. Traffickers and others looking for victims use these sites, too. Facebook, Instagram, and Snapchat are common places for traffickers to search. They gather personal details about their targets. Usernames with a real name or birthday are helpful to them. They also scan users' bios and posts for their ages, locations, and

A person's social media accounts can provide traffickers with the information they need to win over their victim.

schools. It's smart not to offer such details. A person knowing details that the user hasn't shared is a sign of **stalking**.

Traffickers may also send friend requests. Avoiding friend requests from strangers is a good safety step. Older traffickers may pose as young people, using someone else's picture. They may want to talk privately. They may prefer to text or use another app. They will likely suggest their friendship be secret, especially from adults. Traffickers try to make their targets feel special and understood. They may want to send gifts or money. They might ask for pictures, including pictures the targets wouldn't share with parents. They may also send revealing pictures. Finally, they might ask to meet the target in person, alone, and

Online stalking raises anxiety and fear in the teens who experience it.

in secret. Social media users should trust any uneasy thoughts or feelings they have about a person they meet online. Being aware and making smart decisions are good ways to fight trafficking.

GLOSSARY

enslaved

held against one's will and forced to work without pay

exports

sells and sends goods to other places, such as another country

fronts

legal businesses that disguise an illegal one also operating at the same place

grooming

gaining someone's trust or making them dependent with the goal of abusing them

import

to buy and receive goods from other places, such as another country

lured

tricked someone into doing something

stalking

repeatedly watching or following someone to gain power and control over them

SOURCE NOTES

INTRODUCTION: ADRIANA'S STORY

1. Quoted in Sara Sidner, "Old Mark of Slavery Is Being Used on Sex Trafficking Victims," *CNN*, March 14, 2017. www.cnn.com.

CHAPTER ONE: SEX TRAFFICKING

2. Quoted in Imogen Calderwood, "In Her Own Words: 3 Powerful Stories from Former Child Brides," *Global Citizen*, November 22, 2017. www.globalcitizen.org.

CHAPTER TWO: FORCED LABOR

3. Quoted in Juliana Kim, "No Region Is 'Immune' as the Number of People in 'Modern Slavery' Climbs to 50 Million," *NPR*, September 13, 2022. www.npr.org.

4. Quoted in "The Intersection Between Migrant Work and Labor Trafficking," *Laboratory to Combat Human Trafficking*, March 13, 2023. www.combathumantrafficking.org.

CHAPTER THREE: DEBT AND DESCENT SLAVERY

5. Quoted in Faras Ghani, "The Spiraling Debt Trapping Pakistan's Brick Kiln Workers," *Aljazeera*, October 21, 2019. www.aljazeera.com.

CHAPTER FOUR: ENDING SLAVERY

6. Quoted in Francesca Street, "Meet the Abduction Survivor Helping Airlines Stop Human Trafficking," *CNN*, October 17, 2019. www.cnn.com.

FOR FURTHER RESEARCH

BOOKS

Tammy Gagne, *Refugee and Immigrant Rights*. San Diego, CA: BrightPoint Press, 2025.

Lisa Idzikowski, *Human Trafficking*. New York: Greenhaven, 2023.

Philip Wolny, *Gender Violence*. San Diego, CA: BrightPoint Press, 2025.

INTERNET SOURCES

"Buy Slave Free." *End Slavery Now*, 2023. www.endslaverynow.org.

"Report Trafficking." *National Human Trafficking Hotline Polaris*, 2023. www.humantraffickinghotline.org.

"Technology and Human Trafficking: Avoid the Trap!" *United Nations Office on Drugs and Crime*, 2022. www.unodc.org.

WEBSITES

Free the Slaves
www.freetheslaves.net

Free the Slaves gives information about modern slavery. It also provides resources for student activists.

Freedom United
www.freedomunited.org

The Freedom United site is a source for information about modern slavery. It includes videos, webinars, podcasts, and opportunities to join the fight.

100 Million Campaign
www.100million.org

The youth-led 100 Million Campaign invites young people to join an international organization devoted to wiping out child slavery, child labor, and poverty. The site offers information and resources.

INDEX

American Civil War, 9, 41
antislavery organizations, 44, 52

brick kilns, 34–36

child marriages, 19–21, 48
child soldiers, 31
COVID-19 pandemic, 29–32, 46

debt slavery, 32, 34–38
descent slavery, 32, 41–42
domestic workers, 24–26, 30

economic action, 48–52
End Slavery Now, 52
Epstein, Jeffrey, 18

factories, 26, 37
fair trade, 50–52
forced labor, 21, 22–32, 36, 49–52
forced marriages, 19–21, 48

grooming, 15–17

hotlines, 12–14, 28, 54

International Labour Organization (ILO), 14, 21, 25, 31–32, 46

Kozakiewicz, Alicia, 49

Laboratory to Combat Human Trafficking (LCHT), 28

Mauritania, 42
Maxwell, Ghislaine, 18
Me, Angela, 24
migrant workers, 26–28, 30, 38, 48

Napolitano, Kara, 28

online trafficking, 49, 54–57

poverty, 20, 30–31, 37–38, 49

recognizing slavery, 52–54

sex trafficking, 8, 12–18, 25, 48
stalking, 56

United Nations (UN), 11, 24, 44, 46
US slavery, 9, 38, 41

Walk Free, 44
wars, 9, 24, 31, 41, 46

Xinjiang, 49–50

IMAGE CREDITS

Cover: © John Gomez/Alamy
5: © Alan Fraser Images/Shutterstock Images
7: © alexnika/Shutterstock Images
9: © Creativa Images/Shutterstock Images
10: © Marzolino/Shutterstock Images
13: © alexkich/Shutterstock Images
15: © kuzmaphoto/Shutterstock Images
16: © Dragon Images/Shutterstock Images
20: © HM Shahidul Islam/Shutterstock Images
23: © Dragon Images/Shutterstock Images
25: © Red Line Editorial
27: © Tinnakorn Jorruang/Shutterstock Images
29: © Berns Images/Shutterstock Images
33: © Logan Bush/Shutterstock Images
35: © kaikups/Shutterstock Images
37: © Salahuddin Ahmed Paulash/Shutterstock Images
40: © Zvonimir Atletic/Shutterstock Images
43: © Senderistas/Shutterstock Images
45: © John Gomez/Shutterstock Images
47: © Taljat David/Shutterstock Images
51: © Azamat Imanaliev/Shutterstock Images
53: © yonikamoto/Shutterstock Images
55: © Wachiwit/Shutterstock Images
57: © Ground Picture/Shutterstock Images

ABOUT THE AUTHOR

Gail Radley believes books are revolutionary. They touch our hearts and help build our characters. Radley has written over forty books. She lives in Florida with her husband, three big cats, and one little dog. Radley dedicates this book to her daughter, whose tender and caring heart fills her mom with pride.